HAIKU
for
Project Managers

Project Knowledge in Seventeen Syllables

IT'S ALWAYS THE TRUTH
THAT PROJECTS AREN'T EASY
UNLESS WE'RE ALONE

Robert Prol, PMP

Printed in the United States of America

First Printing November 2016

ISBN 978-0-9885839-1-7

Captain Morgan Press
East Sandwich, MA 02537

www.robertprol.com

Contents

Introduction

I'm often asked "what is a Haiku?" when people first stumble across one of my Haiku online. When I asked Google this question, the response was "a Japanese poem of seventeen syllables, in three lines of five, seven, and five". This form of poetry originated in 17th century Japan. It doesn't need to rhyme.

I'd often research a project management topic and find hundreds, if not thousands of potential answers in books, articles, and blogs. Over the years I've purchased books focused on specific project management topics. All of the books could have been summarized in a feature-length article. Most feature-length articles could be summarized in a shorter article. This got me thinking... maybe they could be summarized in something even shorter.

A little over a year ago I challenged myself to publish an original Haiku every work day for a year. I missed about 5 days in that year. A few months into this exercise readers started to ask when I'd publish a book of Haiku. This book is the answer to that question and contains some of my favorites. I hope you enjoy reading them as much as I enjoyed writing and discussing them.

Here's one of my favorite Haiku, written by my friend Frank Calandra:

The Number One myth

About Project Management

Is that it exists

LEADERSHIP

We've all worked for a micro-manager before. They reserve every decision for themselves and in the process make us believe we're incapable of independent thought.

Part of my career in the US Army Reserves was in command and staff training. We'd utilize computer simulations to replicate a battle and then observe and train the staff as they managed the ensuing battle. We'd watch for the "hero", the person who runs from place to place firing off decisions. We'd then "kill" him by removing him from the exercise. The staff would generally fail since they couldn't function without that "hero". The point was made. Teams only work when everyone has a role they can focus on. People also must to be able to function respectably one level above their current position.

The most valuable service we can provide our teams is to help them become confident in their skills. Making decisions for them will negatively impact their confidence. The sign of a great leader is when the leader disappears and the team continues to function.

PMI process: *Develop Project Team*

Build team confidence

Or you'll own all decisions

And your team won't grow

Our initial reaction when a team member is late delivering is to be angry and confront the person. Over the years I've learned that we must approach the person with an open mind and find out if there was a miscommunication in what was expected, or some external factor that impacted the team member. This forces us to look at ourselves as the source of the issue first.

When we identify the issue as residing with a team member our focus must be in coaching our teams through the tough spots, even if they don't report to us. By doing this they'll be more dedicated to us and to the team.

PMI process: *Develop Project Team*

Build your people up

They will be more productive

Than beating them down

Great leaders measure their responses. They speak in positive tones and effectively convey the point they want to make as clearly as possible.

When faced with challenging topics I need to discuss, I write notes to make sure I cover the key points. I then edit them to focus on what we need to do, as opposed to what we didn't do, or did wrong.

People hear what they want to hear. Make sure that none of your words can be misinterpreted.

PMI process: *Direct and Manage Project Work*

Think before you speak

Your words can't be taken back

Once they cause damage

To be successful we must surround ourselves with competent people. Work to identify and support the people who possess leadership qualities and build these qualities in those that may not see their own potential.

Never feel threatened by having competent people working for you, or with you. Success is best when shared.

PMI process: *Develop Project Team*

Go create leaders

Out of people on your teams

There's strength in numbers

People tend to not like changes, or new directions. I've experienced this when implementing new processes or tools. Even a convoluted and inefficient process is comfortable for people who have always done it that way.

It's our responsibility to lead the changes, especially when the opposition gets the noisiest. We must remind our teams, and often ourselves, that the outcome we're working toward is worth the effort.

PMI process: *Direct and Manage Project Work*

Leading is scary

When we first chart a new path

Yet we can't waiver

Not all work is fun. Some of it is boring, repetitive, wasteful, or just dumb. Our first instinct may be to delegate this work. Because "stuff" rolls downhill.

When I come across activities that drain the motivation from me, I first try to redesign process to make the task easier. If that fails then I may take turns completing the activity with others, acknowledging that this isn't fulfilling and likely not needed.

Delegate because the person you're delegating to either has the skill needed, or needs to develop the skill. Don't delegate because the activity isn't fun and you don't want to do it.

PMI process: *Develop Project Team*

Learn to delegate

In ways that enhance the team

Don't just avoid work

I'm always amazed at the tenacity of people working for employers who pay little and have poor benefits. It's usually because they like their boss and the people they work with. Conversely, I've experienced very unhappy people working for what looks like a great company with awesome benefits.

People will persevere in a bad situation because they like the people they work with and their boss. Having a great boss makes Monday mornings feel like sunshine and fresh air. Be the sunshine and fresh air for your team. Make their jobs fun.

PMI process: *Develop Project Team*

People don't quit jobs

But they do quit bad leaders

Make them want to stay

Anyone can lie and manipulate their way through a project once. People will put their doubts aside and work through the dysfunction. They may grumble and complain to their functional manager, but the project manager will likely be provided the opportunity to grow into the role.

The ability to successfully lead not one, but multiple projects over time is what will determine your career success as a project manager.

Padding schedules to make a deadline tells the team you don't trust them. If it's due on Tuesday in 3 weeks, never tell them it's due on Thursday in 2 weeks. It's okay to say you'd like the activity wrapped up by an earlier date to have time to review/absorb/socialize it, but never lie to get a project done quicker. Once trust is broken it can't be restored. I've never had a team upset at me for telling them the truth, even if it hurt.

PMI process: *Direct and Manage Project Work*

Using fake deadlines

As a way to push your teams

Destroys trust in you

MEETINGS

Many projects require us to organize and lead meetings with people at high levels in an organization. We're often forced to look weeks ahead to find a time that works for everyone. After multiple phone calls and emails an invitation goes out. A key person declines the meeting without offering an alternative time. We go back and continue looking for another time slot that works...

This is when I reach out directly to the person to determine if they don't want to meet at all, or if they just can't make that specific time. This often results in the meeting being sooner than we'd originally planned.

Don't wait to manage this type of situation. Act while it's still fresh on their mind.

PMI process: *Direct and Manage Project Work*

Declined my meeting

No alternatives offered

I don't quit easy

$\mathcal{S}$tudies show that meetings start late because other meetings end late. My meetings start at 3 minutes after the scheduled start time. I reschedule if we're still missing a key stakeholder 5 minutes after the start time. I state this policy in my invitations to new project teams. There's no napping in project management. At least not where we may be caught napping.

PMI process: *Monitor and Control Project Work*

I arrived on time

I'm the only one that's here

Can I take a nap?

Work has evolved. We're often assigned more work than we can manage. This forces us to respond to emails and instant messaging while on conference calls.

As project managers we need to evolve our skills to overcome this in ourselves, as well as on our teams. One tactic I utilize is to always do a screen share in a meeting. I may share something as simple as my notetaking. This keeps most attendees focused on the meeting discussion. Ask people questions during the meeting. This will ensure they stay engaged. Release people who may not have a stake in the discussion by having them provide their update first.

When I'm caught multitasking I confess, apologize, and ask for the person to repeat the question. People won't remember this as much as they'll remember a rambling non-answer.

PMI process: *Manage and Control Project Work*

I asked a question

Your answer appears off-base

Caught multitasking?

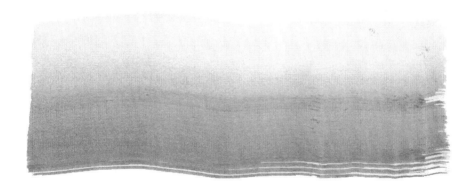

Facilitating effective meetings is one of our most important skills. We need to run them so effectively that our attendees remember that the meeting didn't waste their time.

When a key stakeholder doesn't show up at a meeting I send them an instant message or an email to find out if they plan to attend. If I don't have a response by 5 minutes after the start time, I thank the attendees who did show up, and reschedule the meeting. Nothing shows our respect for our team more than respecting their time.

I usually only do this once on a project, then everyone gets the message that meetings start on time. They also end on time, or even better, they end early. We can all use the break.

PMI process: *Manage Stakeholder Engagement*

I changed my schedule
So we could have your meeting
Maybe you forgot

Some people think that meetings are combat where they must win. There are some meetings where this is true. A meeting to identify a collaborative solution isn't one of these.

Collaborative solutions require that we don't have a pre-set outcome we can't live without. We need to listen to all ideas and find the solution that everyone can support and work with. It's about the team and moving forward, not about who has the best idea.

Building collaborative solution skills are critical for our project management toolkit. The more complex our projects are, the more this skill is required.

PMI process: *Manage Project Team*

Leave your guns outside

We're here to collaborate

Not to see who wins

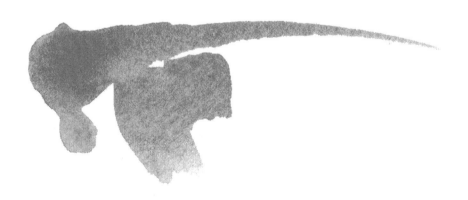

Think about meetings that stand out in your mind. You'll likely remember the ones that were run very poorly and the ones that were awesome. You can probably remember who facilitated these meetings. Be the person who's remembered for the awesome meetings.

Effective meetings are critical to project success. Never send a meeting invitation without an agenda that contains the purpose of the meeting, and the outcome that's needed from it.

Be an assertive facilitator by keeping everyone focused on the agenda. This can be very uncomfortable at times, but no one ever said project management was going to be easy.

Your attendance rate will improve dramatically when you have a reputation for running awesome meetings.

PMI process: *Monitor and Control Project Work*

Meetings are our life

Learn to make them productive

Or remain lonely

I'm sharing this secret with you. Very few people read the meeting notes. All they care about is what they are on the hook to do before the next meeting and what others owe them. Intranet archives are loaded with years of beautifully formatted weekly meeting notes that are rarely opened.

Years ago I modified my notetaking habits. I'm an optimizer who's always looking for the path of least resistance in my work. My notes have the actions up top with the owner's name in bold. Notes are limited to information we need to capture, such as rationale for a decision, changes in direction, information that clarifies a deliverable or provides deeper context in the project.

Avoid writing a "who said what when" log of the meeting. This is way too much information and generally not worth the effort.

PMI process: *Manage Communications*

No one reads the notes

Yet everyone expects them

Make sure they look good

Knowing the right questions is more important than having all the answers. Most project teams have a wide mix of subject matter experts who can be leveraged. Admitting you don't have an answer isn't a sign of vulnerability or weakness. It's a sign that you possess the confidence and competence to lead the team to success.

PMI process: *Monitor and control project work*

I can't know it all

I ask the dumb questions

To learn what I need

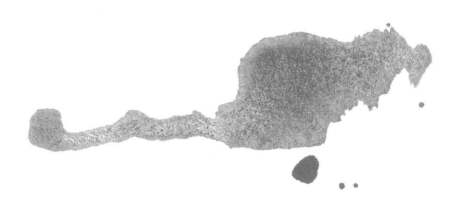

always try to alleviate the administrative load on a team by doing a lot of preparation for meetings. Having documents prepared prior to a meeting makes the meeting easier to facilitate and I leave with the outcome we need.

For project kick offs I always have a scope document ready. Sending the documents out in advance will rarely save you time. Few people will read them before the meeting. Make sure you know the scope well enough to speak to it without reading it to the team.

PMI process: *Validate Scope*

Project scope goes out

The team attends the meeting

Amnesia has struck

always place actions at the top of meeting notes, with each action starting with the owner's name.

Example: **Bob** to distribute the edited scope document by this Friday (11/18)

Depending on who the person is and my available time, I resend the actions to the owners as the next meeting approaches to remind them of their commitments. This is especially important when leadership owes the team something. Confirm they have it before the meeting. If they don't have it consider rescheduling the meeting.

PMI process: *Control Communications*

The notes were sent out

Actions were placed at the top

How did you miss yours?

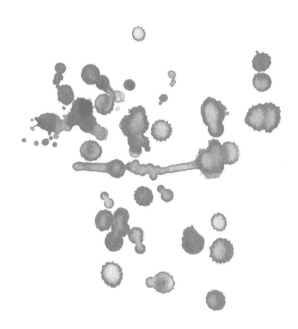

This was one of my least favorite aspects of managing projects early in my career. Everyone would be agreeable in the meeting and we'd leave with decisions. It was later that I'd find out that a member of the team's agreement wasn't truly an agreement.

It took time for me to realize that I was asking people to do something outside of their authority. We were all too inexperienced to know this. They'd go back to their department and their boss would override their agreement. I'd spend time trying to find out how to move a project forward after reporting to my boss that the project was on track.

Knowing who owns decision authority at the start of a project will save us lots of time later. This will decrease finger pointing, inter-departmental disagreements, and many hours of meetings.

PMI process: *Manage Project Team*

The project meetings

Are when we need to speak up

Not when it's over

It's not easy taking notes on a project when the person speaking hasn't organized their thoughts before starting to speak. Trying to listen while capturing the relevant information can provide a lot of stress for a project manager.

There are so many great collaboration tools - like SharePoint and OneNote, that I've converted most of my project teams to "crowd sourcing" our notes. I send out a link to the shared note space and ask attendees to update their notes in advance of meetings. Then I can focus better on facilitating the meeting and capturing action items, without having to unscramble random ramblings.

PMI process: *Manage Project Team*

Make your point clearly

Starting at the beginning

I'm capturing notes

There are many legitimate reasons for someone to show up late to your meetings. I just can't think of any right now. I've had people show up 20 minutes late and want us to start at the beginning of the agenda. *"No"* is my standard response. The notes will catch the person up.

What does it tell the people who showed up on time if you move back to the start of the agenda? That showing up on time doesn't matter.

PMI process: *Control Stakeholder Engagement*

When people are late

Don't punish the attendees

Start meetings promptly

I recommend not accepting a meeting invitation that lacks an agenda. When I receive one of these, I respond as tentative and ask the organizer what the meeting will focus on. There are times when this may not be appropriate or comfortable to address due to the level of the person sending the invitation. Then I accept it to resolve my curiosity around the topic.

One great technique I utilize to focus someone else's agenda-less meeting is to ask what outcome she needs to leave with. There are times when an organizer needs help articulating why we need to meet.

PMI process: *Control Stakeholder Engagement*

Without agendas
We all wander aimlessly
Until the call ends

I attended a virtual training session recently where I was very interested in what the speaker had to say. Unfortunately, he stood far from the microphone. After several fruitless request for him to speak up or move closer to the microphone, I decided he must not have anything important to say.

Facilitating virtual meetings can be challenging. It's our job to make sure everyone can participate productively. Periodically asking the attendees if they can hear is one way to do this. Designate someone in the room to advocate for the virtual attendees, providing them an opportunity to be heard in the room.

PMI process: *Manage Stakeholder Engagement*

Your flawless message

Has completely missed the mark

If I can't hear you

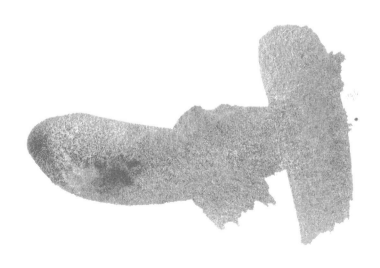

LIFE

Productivity experts speak of "flow". The state of mind where you are blowing through activities without taxing your conscious mind. There's no better flow killer than a meeting for the sake of having a meeting. Look at your calendar and identify how much time you aren't in meetings and can do your work. If it's limited, maybe you need to start asking why you attend (or organize) meetings.

I'm constantly in a quest to optimize my time as well as my project teams' time. This means that I designate a "core team" who I will meet with more frequently. The core team members are expected to interact with their departments and ensure that information and decisions flow to and from the project team. I always try to resolve issues via email unless my emails are ignored.

Sometimes I'll schedule a meeting where I state in the invitation that if my questions can be answered by email we can cancel the meeting. This is very effective in getting responses.

PMI process: *Manage Stakeholder Engagement*

I'm in a nice groove

The next meeting wastes my time

Must I dial in?

Up until about four years ago I avoided connecting my smart phone to work email. My wife and I made the decision twenty years ago that we'd build a life that wasn't work-centric.

This doesn't mean we don't work hard or that we wouldn't do what was needed outside of conventional work hours to ensure success. But most of the work we saw people doing on weekends and at night could easily be done during the day.

I always let my project teams know that I don't check email on weekends. If they send me an email on Saturday morning and they need me to respond or act on the email, they must call or text my mobile phone.

PMI process: *Plan Stakeholder Management*

Your weekend emails

Will be answered on Monday

I'm enjoying life

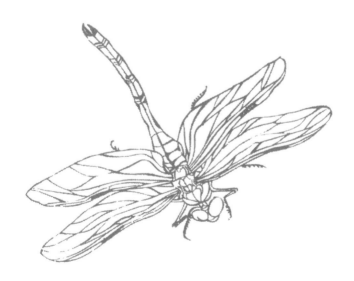

Everyone was born with art skills. We scribbled on paper, mashed clay into lumps vaguely resembling animals, and sang loudly. As we grow up we shift to "serious" stuff. Like how to make money to accumulate stuff.

There's a whole universe of research that proves we need to have interests outside of the office in order to be productive at work. We all need a hobby we can focus on when not doing "serious" stuff.

I play the ukulele, take singing lessons, carve wood, and bird watch. I maintain a physical exercise program. Research shows that the more time we spend at work, the less we accomplish.

When I come across a challenging issue at work I'm likely to change into running gear and take off on a 30-minute run. Or I'll pick up my ukulele and sing *Wagon Wheel* at my home office desk. This usually results in finding a solution before I refocus on the issue.

What's your hobby? What art skill did you lose as you grew up?

PMI process: *Develop Project Team*

Take up a hobby

That isn't work related

You'll get more done

Maybe it's an infantry skill I learned while serving. No matter how bad things are there's always an aspect that's good. When crawling through the mud in a pouring rain I'd think how great it is that the water is warm. Or that the mud hasn't made it to my underwear. Yet.

A few years ago I had a colleague across the cubicle wall from me who liked to engage in short conversations through the wall. We considered ourselves cubicle philosophers. Renaissance men in a nondescript impersonal work space. One day he said "happiness is a choice". I hadn't thought about it that much, but it got me thinking...

The truth is that a happy disposition is contagious. It changes how we view the world and how we perceive the activities around us. Choose to be happy. Life is way more fun when we're happy.

PMI process: *Develop Project Team*

Choose to be happy

You'll find success follows you

And you won't be sad

used to toss and turn all night when work was wearing on me. I'd get up and pace the house. I'd have a snack while lamenting that I was awake all night. This could last days as the issue played out. My performance and focus would degrade as the lack of sleep accumulated.

One day my wife recommended that I confront the issue right away rather than letting it fester. I'd convinced myself that I needed to have a solution before I confronted the issue. Yet what I truly needed to do was include the other person in the discussion. This would allow us to find a solution together.

Getting enough sleep is just as important as eating healthy foods, exercising, and having strong relationships. Actively confront whatever issues make you lose sleep. Your body and brain will thank you.

PMI process: *Manage Project Team*

Get a good night's sleep

Or performance will suffer

And you'll lose more sleep

We work hard and fast all day trying to maintain a pace to match our tremendous amount of work. We're frantic, often making our responses short and pointed. When we arrive back home our pace remains. We exert the same intensity and drive that we carried all day. It's difficult to shift back into a spouse, parent, or friend that we are.

Take a break during the day. Go for a walk outside of the office. Visit a park. People watch. Read a book. The rest of your day will be more productive and you'll be more relaxed when you get home.

PMI process: *Develop Project Team*

I see it from here

A beautiful world outside

I think I'll join it

The year 2016 reminded me of how fragile life can be. I lost a brother-in-law I'd known since I was a young teenager when he started dating one of my sisters. A few months later one of my brothers died unexpectedly of a heart attack. Just a few short months later another brother died in a bicycle accident.

I'm a busy guy. I don't often take the time to call my siblings or to stay in constant touch. We can always catch up at the next family function. Sadly most of our family functions this year were funerals for people I love.

Say "I love you" more and be free with your hugs with people who matter to you. Just not at work, because hugging may not be appropriate there.

PMI process: *Develop Project Team*

Life can end real fast

Someone else will do your work

Hug your family now

In 2010 I had high cholesterol, high blood pressure and high triglyceride levels. I was thirty pounds overweight and frequently sick. My doctor handed me a stack of statin samples and a prescription for more. She wanted to see me in a few months and then we'd address my high blood pressure. I asked what I could do to avoid taking medicine. She told me to take the meds. I wouldn't be able to manage this alone.

I did my research and changed my diet. I knocked the dust off my running shoes. Three months later my cholesterol was close to normal, my triglyceride levels were normal and I'd lost about 10 pounds.

Today my BMI is normal, as are all my health indicators. I rarely get sick. My energy levels are very high and I sleep great.

Our health is the most important thing we can focus on to have a fulfilling life. Money, position, the size of our home, the car we drive means nothing if we're struggling with our health.

PMI process: *Develop Project Team*

Manage your health first

Being sick doesn't help you

Deliver on time

When it comes to work life balance people will emulate the leaders in an organization. Many organizational cultures avoid any discussion of what they do outside of work. I'm not saddled with that problem.

Some of the interesting things my colleagues engage in are owning and managing a car race team, writing for Huffington Post, competing in Spartan races, running marathons, performing in bands and volunteering at soup kitchens.

It's all these personal connections that will help the team through the tough times. It'll also help them validate that they are human and their interests have value among their colleagues. Acknowledge their life outside of the office by speaking of yours and asking about their life.

PMI process: *Develop Project Team*

Connect with your team

By treating them as humans

Who enjoy their lives

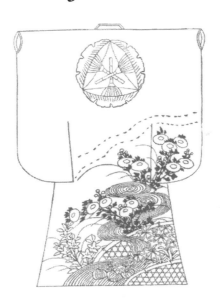

started attending college when I was almost 30 years old. Up until then I owned a landscape construction business. My work days were outside in all weather, installing retaining walls, sidewalks, and plantings. I loved being outside and working with my hands. I could see progress and it was clear when a project was complete. Some days I miss the feel of the sun on my face, dirt on my hands, and sense of accomplishment when seeing the results of my efforts.

I can't figure out if the squirrels are happy or not, but they are outside and I'm not. They never watch me watch them so I assume they're happy.

PMI process: *Develop Project Team*

View from my office

Squirrels running in the trees

No concern for me

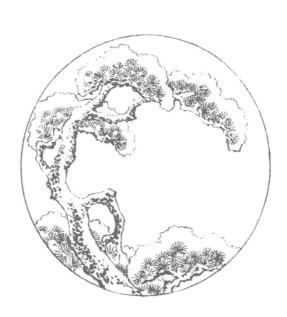

Every day of the week has some theme to it. Wednesday is "Hump Day". Thursday is almost Friday. Friday is when we look forward to the weekend. The weekend needs no theme. Monday is to be dreaded since it's our first day back to work after the weekend. What is Tuesday?

I was mobilized with the US Army Reserve in 2003 and we worked weeks-on-end with no time-off in sight. I commented one day that every day for us was a Tuesday. The days just blended. It struck a chord with the team. Tuesdays have never been the same for me since then.

PMI process: *Develop Project Team*

What is a Tuesday?

Just another day to work

Far from both weekends

FOCUS

I've often observed that the people who walk around talking to other people all day are the same ones who work late because they have "so much to do". Or they stay late, then pack a rolling suitcase to bring work home with them to keep the fun going. I've experienced downsizing several times in my career and these extra hours make no difference when layoffs start.

I once had a boss who would schedule 7:00 PM meetings in his office. I attended the first one, my stomach growling to match my mood. The next time he scheduled one of these I proposed an alternate time of 7:00 AM the next day. He rarely made it to the office before 10:00 AM. I knew it wouldn't happen. He responded that he couldn't meet that early since he has breakfast with his children. It's their tradition. I replied that I couldn't meet at 7:00 PM because I have dinner with my wife. It's our tradition. He suddenly found time during the day to meet.

PMI process: *Monitor and Control Project Work*

Do your work all day

Focus on what's important

You'll be home on time

Being busy is different than getting things done. Choose your priorities each day and then focus on them until they're complete. The constant distractions of email and instant messaging will rob you of productivity. This is called the cost of shifting focus. Each time we change from one issue to the next we lose about 15 minutes of productivity.

I work in blocks of time. I don't check email or deviate from a specific project activity until it's complete. I find that about 30 minutes of focusing on a project works out just about right. This also makes tracking my time against each project much easier.

PMI process: *Monitor and Control Project Work*

Get self-discipline

Or let each activity

Drive you from your goal

Our job isn't to answer emails; it's to be productive. Email is a tool that assists us in being productive. Answering every email as soon as it arrives will draw you away from your daily goals.

This is the same for instant messaging. I always leave mine on unless it starts to get too distracting. Then I turn it off until I'm ready to move on to a new action, at which time I check my emails and turn on my instant messaging.

PMI process: *Monitor and Control Project Work*

I planned my whole day

It was to be productive

Then I checked email

I live by an "Inbox Zero" creed. I never leave work for the day with an unopened email. If I can answer the email in less than two minutes, I do this. If it will take longer, I flag it for follow up and respond that I read the email. I let them know when to expect a response. I then follow up based on what I committed to.

A few years ago I was waiting days for a response from a development lead. I sent a follow up. A few days later I sent another follow up.

I stalked him. It's something I reserve the right to do. When I found where he sat in our sprawling office complex, he said he hadn't seen my email or either of the follow ups. I spied his inbox and saw that he had over 2,000 unread emails. I would guess that his inability to triage his email meant that he had the same request multiple times, which added to his backlog.

It's your responsibility to make your boss aware if you have too much work.

PMI process: *Monitor and Control Project Work*

You're not effective

With countless unread emails

Learn how to triage

THAT PERSON

Few organizations manage resources or prioritize projects well. This means they have little insight into each person's workload. Project managers are often competing against other project managers or other work their team members are assigned to.

If an organization doesn't set priorities, then by default all work is low priority. This is because the full portfolio of activities are randomly prioritized by each person across the full range of projects.

It's in our best interest to know what other projects our team members are working on and how they are prioritizing that work. When you disagree with a team member's priorities, involve other project managers she is working with to come to a consensus on the organization's priorities. Never leave a team member to fend for themselves in prioritizing her workload.

PMI process: *Manage Project Team*

CRITICAL PROJECT!

You don't seem to really care

Sleeping at your desk

Not all decisions in a project can be based on a clear set of data. This is where our professional judgment becomes critical. When we're early in our careers we may not have the experience needed to exercise good judgment. This is when we need to rely on a coach or a mentor to help us develop judgment. Over time we will develop the ability to quickly assess a situation and come up with the best course of action. We should consider a different career path if we don't develop sound judgment.

A project manager must know who owns the decision in any given situation. We shouldn't make decisions we don't own. Instead we must rely on the decision owner.

PMI process: *Control Scope*

Follow your instincts

Unless you don't have any

Then just follow mine

The best place to learn project management is in a dysfunctional organization. It forces us to develop the ability to identify and manage dysfunctional behavior, as well as our confrontation skills.

I learned a valuable lesson early in my career. A new vice president was brought in to lead our department. When I met with her I related my irritation at a director on another site. She asked me how that he responded when I talked to him about it. I hadn't talked to him about it, so her point was made. Later in my career when I had someone on my team come to complain about someone else, I asked her if I could bring the other person into the conversation now, or did they want to talk to that person first. I was willing to help both of them work through their issues after they made an attempt first. She quickly left my office and the issue never came up again.

We can't allow ourselves to endorse dysfunction. Be the beacon of sanity, not a combatant in the swamp.

PMI process: *Direct and Manage Project Work*

Here comes the big bus

Be sure to push very hard

On guilty one's back

I believe in treating people as I want to be treated. If that fails I treat them like they treat me. This is a very useful skill that I only implement on rare occasions and only in private with that person. It's especially helpful when the person refuses to engage with me in finding common ground and moving forward. I think of it as mirroring, or reflecting them back at themselves.

This isn't an entry level skill. It's most effective when dealing with a bully in the workplace or someone who is continuously impeding progress. I use this sparingly.

PMI process: *Manage Project Team*

I do have filters

But I choose not to use them

When talking to you

I'm often surprised by the people I've never worked with or met who endorse my skills on LinkedIn. Knowing what I do for a living is much different than knowing if I'm good at it.

When it comes to endorsing others I am very careful who I endorse, and how I endorse them. If I wouldn't say something positive about the person with someone we both worked with, or directly to the person, I wouldn't post it publicly. I decline requests for endorsements for people I never worked with.

PMI process: *Control Stakeholder Engagement*

I have endorsements

From connections I don't know

Unrequited love?

Most projects teams are virtual. We can't walk to someone's workspace and ask a question, instead relying on instant messaging, email and phone calls.

Getting someone's attention and response isn't always easy. Sometimes the person is a key stakeholder and very high up in an organization. We may be hesitant to ask for a response to an email we already sent. This can cause delays in a project.

My tactics to get an answer run on a sliding scale based on the time available:

- A follow-up email
- A voice message
- A carefully crafted meeting invitation, where I state that if I can have my answer before the meeting, we can cancel the meeting
- Forward the email chain to their boss expressing concern that maybe the person is out for an extended period.

That last step always gets an answer, an apology, and their future attention.

PMI process: *Monitor and Control Project Work*

I sent five emails

No one responded to me

I will send five more

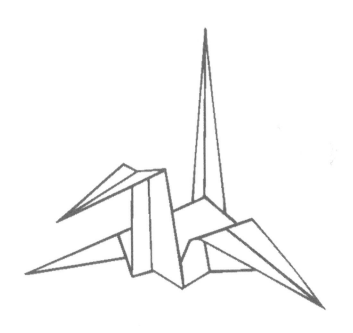

Projects range from very simple and clear to very complex and plagued with ambiguity. Project managers tend to know the types of projects they like. Not all of us like the simple and clear projects.

Those who can't tolerate ambiguity should choose another career field. My passion is in managing complex projects where the requirements aren't clear and the path to completion needs to be mapped with the team. This is where I can apply my skills to lead the team to a successful outcome.

When people complain about project management, I remind them that if it were easy they wouldn't be needed. Jobs that don't require human judgment will be replaced by robots or artificial intelligence. Don't be replaced by a robot. Be proud of your career choice. Embrace the complexity. The simple projects will be executed by robots.

PMI process: *Develop Project Management Plan*

If it were easy

We wouldn't be in this role

So stop complaining

A good project manager's most valuable reward is the feeling we get inside from a project executed well. We rarely get the credit when a project is a success. Find a different career path if you need constant reassurance of your value.

Anyone can successfully manage a project once. It's the ability to be successful not once, but multiple times with many of the same team members that separates the project management hobbyists from the professionals. Creating a team culture, sharing the success, and assuming responsibility for failures is an attribute we must possess if we make project management our career.

Superheroes don't need to brag. Their successes speak for themselves.

PMI process: *Control Stakeholder Engagement*

Project managers

Aren't your superheroes

We just act like it

A great team works like a great marriage. We must remain committed in the good times, and especially in the bad times. Sacrificing a team member when they make a mistake impacts the trust of the team.

We must take the time to understand why a team member continuously misses deadlines and help him resolve the underlying issues. It may be his workload, how he prioritizes or his lack of understanding of the tasks. Coaching him through the tasks will develop his skills and set the team up for future success. It also creates a bond with the person you're helping, further enhancing team performance.

We also should note when a team member lacks the capacity to do the work and take appropriate action. Since we don't have direct authority over resources on our teams, this often requires us to involve their boss in the discussion. Letting an underperformer continue on a team will drag the team down and adversely impact the project.

PMI process: *Develop Project Team*

We work as a team

Until you miss a deadline

Then it's all your fault

Leading means being able to manage conflict. We're often faced with the decision to allow a team to move forward in the wrong direction or step in to keep it on track. These subtle shifts in direction are often hard to see. We may not think they're worth confronting. As a leader we should always be ready and willing to step in and guide the team in the right direction.

Emotions provide the color and flavor of life. They have only a small place in decision-making.

PMI process: *Monitor and Control Project Work*

My disagreement

Isn't based on my feelings

It's because I'm right

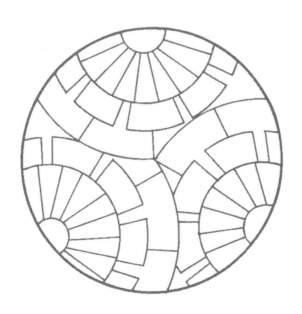

Acknowledgements

This all started as a way to make snarky comments in the office where I was working. I'd post an occasional Haiku on the whiteboard in my cubicle. Due to its prominent location people would stop by to read them, laugh, and talk about meaning of the Haiku. I started to post them on LinkedIn, Facebook, Twitter, and ProjectManagement.com. Then Elizabeth Harrin of @pm4girls fame asked if she could feature a few of my Haiku for National Poetry Day. Thank you Elizabeth for creating the Haiku monster I am.

Special thanks to my wife Rachel Avenia who is the person who makes sure I pursue my passions. She finds ukulele lessons, singing lessons, and woodcarving lessons for me to attend. She also created the cover, internal design, and did all the layout for this book. When I started to assemble the Haiku, she noted that they each needed a description as well as an index to PMBoK.

Special thanks to Frank Calandra. He's always available to bounce ideas off and can be counted on to provide his candid feedback on all matters. He along with Chip Hammond and Glenn Morshauser reviewed layouts, pricing strategy, and other topics for me. I truly appreciate their assistance.

To the many online readers from LinkedIn, Twitter, Facebook, and ProjectManagement.com, thanks for your engagement reading the Haiku. For asking questions, pushing back when I may have missed a syllable, and trying your own hand at Haiku.

Will there be a Second Edition? Probably.

Index

Robert Prol

About the author

Robert Prol is a project manager in the financial services industry. He's managed projects and built and led project management offices in multiple industries. He has held the Project Management Professional certification since 2004 and has a Masters of Science Management degree from Thomas Edison State University and a Masters Certificate in Project Management from Stevens Institute of Technology.

He served 23 years in the US Army National Guard and US Army Reserve where his assignments ranged from a staff driver, operations specialist, scout platoon team leader, bridge specialist in an engineer platoon (he was encouraged to blow things up), a staff trainer and an infantry first sergeant. He retired as a master sergeant in 2004.

He lives close to a beach on Cape Cod, Massachusetts with his wife Rachel and their two feline fuzzballs of love, Shadow and Scoot. When not managing projects or spinning a Haiku, he runs, bikes, carves wood, plays his ukulele (while singing slightly off-key) and birds.

You can connect with him on LinkedIn, Twitter, ProjectManagement.com, RobertProl.com or his Amazon Author's page.

Made in the USA
Columbia, SC
16 May 2017